Money wonder

Exa Axl

"Great appreciation to all that making this E-book happen, the courage and the thought, in making this book I hope it help a lot of young millennial out there help to finance themselves. Finance management and money no one was willing to teach without the effort your willing to put in. It never too late to start anything, the gifts all is out there but no one has the will power to even reach the destination".-Exa Axl

Contents

1.1   The mind work Wonder?

On my second years in university, money makes me wonder how it does make someone feel. How does this amount could multiple it even without searching or working for. Leisure life it is what everybody dream of to be, but I'm different it never happen it my life once to ever ask for money.

Parent always can guess what certainly her daughter need I guess, that how I began to know that the power of money when I'm learning the course of account in my University years. I'm observing people close to me, how society makes those or rich make ton of money with little effort.

Never knew that one of the closer friends of mine come from richest family which I pretty, can sense the way of habit of spending not like the other common people will behave. That are those generation of X and Y, that including me who are always slaughter the Baby boomer money.

Μονεψ Ωονδερ?

1.1   The mind work Wonder?

Talking of her spending, it is not about how she spends on all foods, make up but she speeding on the things that can make her own self-income without any helps. The rate of successful business woman at Terengganu quite high, not sure the reason but when you come to Kuala Terengganu just a few of Man run their business. Lucky enough I've been surrounding with friends that had mind of business, all of them had their own small platform of making money. Indirectly spread that positive vibe in me and help me setup one.

Listening those idea of how making money somehow it really no jokes. I've taken seriously as a drop-shipping agent that the easy way for me to make money since I had a lot of internet access to sold cloths, bag to others teenager as well at student price.

That is no operating cost which profit margin 100%, but you must had continued of the promotion, latest trends and marketing your website. Since Marketing always help you promoting a ton of new peoples, start talking nice to random people could somehow actually be your best friend that how it happens for me.

1.1 <u>The mind work Wonder?</u>

I've learned that if you had pretty a lot of sources of well, one way you can make by trading which most of business out there do. It easy and straight forward business but in the long run it would start to lose the sparks, trend, economic and pattern, that are how the span life of the trading business.

1.2   Making How Happen Reality

Dream as Solo traveller always been on my thoughts several years ago back then before I'm graduating my university years. It becoming my dream even since when I'm reading books a lot of quote stating that such young ages should explore more to see world out there, how world really works. It can be good or bad experience that which we can share to others who never been there, it may trigger somebody to starting having that thought.

After graduating, I got my first jobs to be Audit assistant with earning of RM1, 400 in 2013 which equivalent to USD 300 bucks that really little. Reality works out there is damn hard to meet, to gain a lot of earning they demand us to be experience enough which it is difficult. Regard the earning I only could able survive just nice cover my expenses but it really hard to save more.

In the thought of should I buried the dream of mine because it really hard to save even few hundred when I travelled forth and back from home and office that spend petrol cost a lot on my journey to office and client place too. But anyways it doesn't stop me, I'm start aiming which country that I would think of to be good start off my solo traveler.

1.2   <u>Making How Happen Reality</u>

Searching all information over google seen on all the point of interest places, I decided to choose Japan as my first destination began my solo journey and at the same time choose that autumn weather it should be just nice to me.

Here it began the story how I start saving for my solo Journey. After deciding the place, I want to go, every night and days I always on and off mode see the airline website observe the promotion. After few months watch dogs how the airline cheap price working, I start taking initiate using monthly paid salary to buy the first return ticket. I've notice Air Asia at that time would start doing promotion on Tuesday and Thursday, the others day ticket are super expensive.

If you could wait patiently there will be always had promotion for Air Asia free seat which the price super crazy, some its half of the price. But I'm not choosing that way, since the promotion time only had limited time travel period which mostly likely I can buy the ticket but the travelling period is 1 months after but I don't have the money to spend on my accommodation, sight-seeing and entrance tickets all sort of things.

1.2   Making How Happen Reality

Therefore, I bought ticket advance 6 months which the ticket price is superb cheap, which only cost RM730 plus not including luggage. That how the idea of backpacking start since I dint bought the luggage I need to aware what kind of cloths and trousers I needed to wear instead wear some fancy cloths because back to my first motivation, to see the world closely. Successfully bought the ticket return, I quickly apply leave for vacation and start those researches on itinerary how I'm going spent my 8 days at foreign country, what the thing I need to see, eat, or even the brought back souvenir.

In order to know how much, I need to save for the upcoming vacation, I need to research on how much it costs for entrance, foods, transportation cost and accommodation cost and how much cost to have souvenir, what the local interest places. Every research makes me quite interesting regarding the places, I'm collecting all the information and even do the mapping in order to help myself in advance to save me from getting lost in Japan. Since Wi-Fi usage are open to the public but there is some place can't get through with the Wi-Fi. I've learned some of the language that make me easy to interact with local.

1.2   <u>Making How Happen Reality</u>

The duration of 6 months does help in order to save RM2, 300 that equivalent to USD 550 bucks. On tight budget, packing meals to works was the first choice made up. Another way is by work overtime the paid are considerable good enough for me this idea has made me adventure the whole new idea as a solo traveler, which this idea was previously oppose by family member because of the danger of outside. I acknowledge that somehow human being are afraid for the unknown fear for no reason in fact that actually we all can left behind the worries "Hakuna Matata"

When we're still young, there a lot of overflow energy come out that somehow, we need some reason in order to suit the need of the energy, don't waste energy on something you can't even get benefit nor advantage from its.

1.3   Passive income

After start graduating and had my first jobs, I've had abandoned the small business platform because too lazy and exhausted to run it anyways. Somehow the thought of someone paying me making stop the mind wonder about money whereabouts, in which I somehow regret of not making it happen.

All billionaire and millionaire out there do have their multiple source of income. Depend too much on one source of income it riskier ever, cannot survive and never ever be rich and will always in the same position. Never uplift of yourself, we just living accord to what parent and society thought of how the world is work. It such cruel world, we only try to survive safely by had the stable jobs but in fact it never enough for some fresh grad to even survive in the City expensive lifestyle.

If you see, adulthood these days I believe none of them had even met the failure. The failure maker profile is somehow all the one who are the most successful person in world, such Ali baba, Robert Kiyosaki and many more out there. The lesson is daring enough to fail yourself again and again in order for you to see the failure is opportunity.

1.3   Passive income

That how the importance to making multiple source of income, considering that thought through my full-time service I have gain customer for my Freelance accounting since I'm certified license-chartered accountant. Every review of transaction account got me USD 20 buck each time go there. But I always meet the deadline.

Since audit work has taken a lot of my private time and space, and find myself still working more than it should be that make myself sick, no happiest and got really stress out and sick. Doctor give me relax pills for me which he thought that his afraid of me going crazy and such see things and kill own self, that the reason I gave up because it effects of my health.

But this does not make me stop to had thought of multiple income, I do sign up for I panel account, to do the survey gain free money and I do subscribe investment through ASB (trusted investment limited to Malay) which yield of the dividend quite high each year. Let believe, money is multiple by itself., a year of waiting January finally I could somehow see dividend which are RM6, +++ that would be equivalent estimated USD 2,800. That is really passive that make me happy every year, but this investment does loss some money after time accord to market investment.

1.4   <u>Debts restructuring</u>

Since I had fulltime job, monthly paid had stop my brain work on money. The thought of receiving money doesn't meet my desire on luxury things. But it got more worse when I had credit card facility this had been given the function too keep spending even my monthly paid salary can't afford.

Spending behavior got worse when I'm using it a lot to pay all the utility, travel accommodation and many sorts of things. That at one point, I've been chasing around by banks because skipped one-time payment of monthly instalment. Owe money with banks it really bad idea, I has no idea that bank could even trace down and harass at your work place even

I've telling only that month I've skipped paying because at the time moment I had use my little saving to pursue Scuba diving license which I never proud of having that license. Barely paid below the minimum card spending which bank doesn't allow somehow, bank can wait till payday's time. This is really taking my breath away, that I've never been ever alive over such mistake I've made. These mistakes are causes from spending behavior and bad financial management that I instantly could destroy my own life.

1.4   <u>Debts restructuring</u>

The total debts accumulated my whole ration assets at that time point it is 60 per cent of my income and saving accounts. Negative cash flow few months it really hard, no one should be blame for my terrible spending. I've could ask family members about my situation but I dint. Never dare to bring myself to said those things, it too shameful.

Regardless of what happen I've taken all point to consider and measure properly decided to settle all the mess by my own. It time to consider practice audit skills to on my financial management. I've put goal to achieve free debts and start having control and build my own wealth being.

Admit it was difficult, to saving with little money making from the pay checks. I barely live by pay checks to pay checks because my debts, I've got few personal loan, credit card loan and education loan, to save a lot was not the best idea at times.

I've starting making list, what currently assets and liabilities I hold, how much the liquidity and the debt ratio. Calculated my upcoming salary, I've made monthly budget so I can use my salary according to my plan "Free debts". Priority the debts accord to the interest rate and the due line of the payment.

1.4   Debts restructuring

The financial planner shown as per below, it is the simple and the best work for me. I make sure keep in view these things a lot in weeks, it just reminds myself I can finally remove myself from the burden I had put myself into.

Saving Goal: 10X, XXX (2years) - free debts and save up too

Assets:

1. Car: XXXXX
2. PRS :   XXXXX
3. EPF :   XXXX
4. Cash and banks :

    XXXX Total   XXxXx

Debts:

1. Education loan : XXXX- Auto debit 1st month

2. Credit Card :   XXXX- Due date 14th – interest rate 18%

3. Personal loan : XXXX- Due date 1st Month- interest rate 24%

1.4   Debts restructuring

Monthly commitment (Only all items successfully paid out can fully cross then can be revise)-

1. Telephone post-paid : XX

2. Unifi post-paid : XX

3. Rent room : XX

4. P.A Insurance: XX

5. Education loan : XX

6. Family donation Fund : X

7. Parent Pocket Money : XXX

8. Credit Card : XXX

9. Personal loan : XXX

   Total commitment: XXXX

When each time thinking to take any new commitment even small amount, you should consider amount per year (let said rental of coffee machine 50 dollar (600 dollar per year needed) are you willing to spend that much. Let have that thought consider 1 days and might be needed to drag the desire till 30days. If still insist on buying go for it, it's your pleasure.

1.4   <u>Debts restructuring</u>

Summary of monthly income:

    Salary: XXXXX

    Less commitment:

    (XXXX) Other income:

    XXXX

    Food and transport allowance: XXX

    Net Gross: XXX

Only the net gross the amount that I can spent own anything, but I use to carefully spend on the precious money. I use the rules of per hour's payday in to spend to things. If the products are not work of my 1 hours of working paid, I'm not consider to buy even it tempting me.

1.5   Financial freedom

New principles set up in order to achieve free debts:

- Only priority need over than wants

    o Able to differentiate need and wants it really helpful when making groceries shopping rather than relentless spending

- Paid the debts which had higher interest rate

    o The key it is to paid the debts with 25% of you pay checks, this can help short the time frame of paid a lot of the interest to the banks.

- Saving emergency money out from monthly pocket money

    o I've always saved certain notes (RM5), that easy not big enough and not small enough sometimes I dint wonder if I got lost such amount, because the amount immaterial

    o To accumulate the immaterial amount from your pocket money, at the end of the month always deposit the final amount to banks, you will shock how better you are on saving

1.5   **Financial freedom**

- Financial budget monthly to keep in view each time

    o The budget monthly I've review over and over more than 10 times monthly, I always making sure whether I able to make it out till next paid if I'm sorting this out

    o Should I sort another alternative to support the decision of every budget I need to put on

    o What kind rules this month apply to me that I need to follow

- Never use credit card if don't have the cash money

    o If u have no cash in your hand nor in the bank don't dare to

    swipe the card

    o You should acknowledge "no money meaning your poor and no money no deal"

    o It always win-win situation, if you got the money use credit card, then you paid back getting cash back make you save few bucks, from having to paid two times of the thing your purchase

    o If let said you saw the dream of computer sold at 300 bucks promotion, you will consider to buy it but you had no money

1.5   <u>Financial freedom</u>

that time. Think that 300 bucks should add up the interest you need to bear in daily basic to wait up till someday you finally can pay back the money which might cause 500 bucks, that expensive!

- Fixed deposit few bucks to secure or lock the money to prevent self- spending habits
  - o This is the last method I've used over myself to control my

    spending behavior
  - o Since I know the left over for net gross always triggers me to go

    shopping bought "wants" said as rewards to myself
  - o No such rewards needed when u need to build financial wealth
  - o The lock period 12 months, 3 months really help you settle down the desire and the reality get on you

1.5   <u>Financial freedom</u>

Diversity of income is needed recover from huge debts. I've used my pocket money exchange half of it's to other foreign currency. Time do helps you to gain realised exchange money. Another way it is, this are very passive earn no claim bonus from personal accident insurance that I subscribe previous year, although it not much but it does help me paid the portion of the debts I acquire.

Soon afterward, it was successful paid of my personal loans in just 10 months. I saw the successful make me a lot of happies, finally I could relief that how it works every time. I've become belief to the method that applying to myself. From 60 per cent of debt ratio goes down to 33 per cent of debt ratio over the assets I hold it up.

It never easy to saving and build up the wealth at some point, when you finally see how it works you can plan ahead upcoming days without worries.

The Money Wonder series just one of the first series release to young people out there to realise the important of its. Many young people out there hard to reach or even listen the other people advice.

Seeking help from the expert do need a lot of money, in order to achieve a lot of the other thing free it creates by your own self. It always okay to fall thousand time but make sure to wake it up far stronger than before.

I've created this book in thought that could help arise the awareness of the money. Keeping ask yourself whether did you save enough for your own self expense. Aware of a lot people dint take money as serious object of discussion or put as subject of interest.

In order to archive many greatest things one of its wealth. Build wealth usually come from the proper financial planned that had setup from the beginning. The richest person spent so well not because there having a lot of money to spend off but to see whether the money it returns to them.

It like a cycle that one-person control of the power over and over, now it is the best time even though your not ready. Don't let it sit in the bucket list put the goal in front of you, somehow you finally set the path route your seeking for.

I've been badly and mess up financial management in two years ago, but finally manage it well and start living ambitiously. Getting involve a lot of seminar, books it does help me build over my corrupt of soul. Living on is the only option that need to bear with it, at some point will see that result sooner too.

Decide on finance myself well is one of the best things I could proud of myself. I bring the bad thing out from my own self and polish to be the good diamond. I believe that in you might have a lot of determination and sources than me to create your own too.

Hoping days this E-book could helping you figure it out the financial management yours, do drop email (_fz_eza@yahoo.com_) if you success make it out.

The End, Wait for 2nd Series in the Making.

Thanks for the reading.